Reference Source Data for
GCNP Noise Model Validation Study

Gregg G. Fleming
Christopher J. Roof
Amanda S. Rapoza
David A. Senzig

U.S. Department of Transportation
Research and Special Programs Administration
John A. Volpe National Transportation Systems Center
Acoustics Facility, DTS-34
Cambridge, MA 02142-1093

May 2000
Letter Report DTS-34-FA065-LR2

U.S. Department of Transportation

Research and Special Programs Administration

1. Introduction

The U.S. Department of the Interior (DOI), National Park Service (NPS), and the U.S. Department of Transportation (DOT), Federal Aviation Administration (FAA) are jointly sponsoring a study to examine the accuracy of existing models used for predicting tour aircraft noise in Grand Canyon National Park (GCNP). In particular, three models will be included in the study: the NPS' Noise Overflight Decision Support System (NODSS), the FAA's Integrated Noise Model (INM), and a third model, the Noisemap Simulation Model (NMSIM), which has been developed with funding from both the U.S. Air Force and the National Aeronautics and Space Administration. A key component of the GCNP Noise Model Validation Study is the collection of field data to support the validation effort. These field data will be translated into formats usable by the three noise prediction models. This common set of high quality field data will allow an unbiased comparison of the three models. This letter report addresses portions of the field data collection activity and associated data analysis.

During the daytime hours of September 10, 12 and 13, 1999, a contingent of acoustic researchers conducted measurements at 44 locations in the vicinity of the Zuni Flight Corridor, which generally runs north-to-south in GCNP. A detailed description of the corridor can be found on the most current version of the GCNP VFR aeronautical chart. These researchers included individuals from the NPS, the FAA, Wyle Laboratories (Wyle), Harris Miller Miller and Hanson Inc. (HMMH), and the Volpe Center Acoustics Facility (Volpe). This letter report presents the acoustic data collected at one of the Volpe sites, designated as the Source Site. It also discusses aircraft observation data which were collected simultaneously at the Source Site and at a second Volpe site designated as the Cape Final Site. Figure 1 presents the location of the two Volpe sites relative to the Zuni Flight Corridor. As can be seen, the Source Site (Source) is directly beneath the Zuni Flight Corridor on the South Rim of GCNP, and the Cape Final Site (Cape) is approximately three miles to the west of the corridor on the North Rim.

Section 1 of this letter report presents a brief overview of the study. Section 2 presents a description of the Source Site layout, along with an overview of the instrumentation utilized. Section 3 documents the development of the reference acoustic data to be used in the study. Section 4 documents the reference speed data. Section 5 presents a comparison of the noise-versus-distance (N-D) data developed as part of this effort, with that used in previous GCNP modeling efforts. Appendix A overviews the data contained within the summary spreadsheet used to develop the reference information required for input to the three computer models. Appendix B contains example reference spectral time history data which will be used for input to NMSIM. Appendix C contains reference N-D data which will be used for input to INM. Appendix D contains reference spectral data which will be used for input to NODSS. An Excel spreadsheet containing sound level data is included with this letter report.

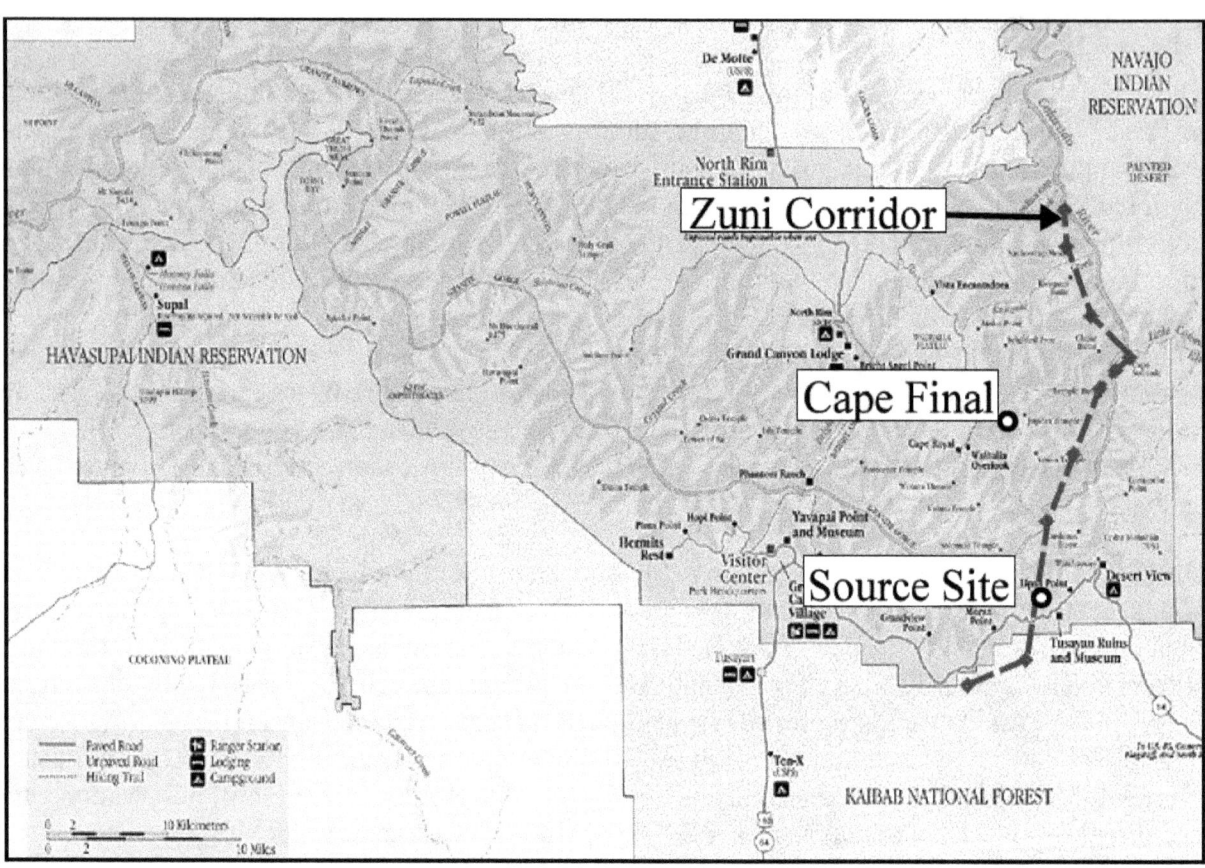

Figure 1. Location of Volpe Source and Cape Final Sites Relative to Zuni Flight Corridor

2.   Description of Source Site Layout and Instrumentation Utilized

Successful collection of reference aircraft data at the Source Site was deemed critical to the overall success of the GCNP noise model validation study. During the planning phase of the study, the Source Site was carefully selected to provide the highest-quality, and most representative reference data for input to the three models. Section 2.1 overviews the Source Site layout, including the characteristics of the site which made it conducive to collection of reference aircraft noise data. Section 2.2 overviews the acoustic instrumentation utilized at the Source Site. Section 2.3 overviews the video tracking system used to obtain aircraft time-space-position information (TSPI) at the Source Site. Section 2.4 overviews some ancillary equipment used at the site.

2.1   Source Site Layout

Figure 2 displays a graphic of the general Source-Site Layout. It also includes the relative coordinate system used for data reduction and the relative position of the three microphones and video tracking systems utilized. The three-microphone array was oriented perpendicular to the north-to-south running Zuni Flight Corridor. The microphones were designated as 1, 2, and 3, where 1 was the western-most microphone, 2 was referred to as the centerline microphone, and 3 was the eastern-most microphone. The spacing between the East and West microphone was approximately 1500 ft. The signals from the three microphones were fed to an instrumentation station located approximately 100 ft to the south of the centerline microphone. The two video tracking systems, one facing east and one facing west, were setup approximately 200 ft to the east of the western-most microphone (Microphone 1). An aircraft observer was stationed at the approximate location of the video cameras.

2.2   Acoustic Instrumentation

Brüel & Kjær (B&K) Model 4155 and 4189 electret condenser microphones were used to convert sound pressure variations into electrical signals. B&K Model 2671 preamplifiers and Deltatron Model WB 1372 power supplies were employed with each microphone. A B&K Model UA0207 foam windscreen was placed atop each microphone to minimize the effects of wind-generated noise on the sound level measurements. The microphone/preamplifier/windscreen combination was fixed on a tripod at a height of 4 feet above the ground. On-line acoustic data were recorded for the three Source Site microphones on Larson Davis Model 820 real-time integrating sound level meters. One-second equivalent sound level ($L_{Aeq,1s}$) data were measured. Data were also recorded, for archival purposes and off-line analysis, on Sony PC208Ax, digital audio tape (DAT) recorders. Each DAT tape was encoded with IRIG B timecode to aid in off-line analysis. Figure 3 below presents an example of this instrumentation set-up in the field, while Figure 4 presents a block diagram of the system.

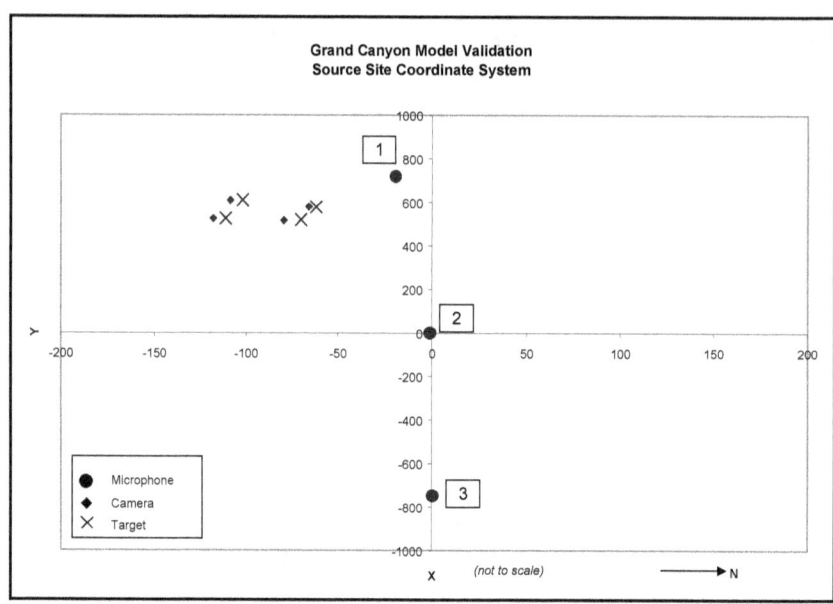

Figure 2. Overview of Source Site Layout

Figure 3. Acoustic Instrumentation

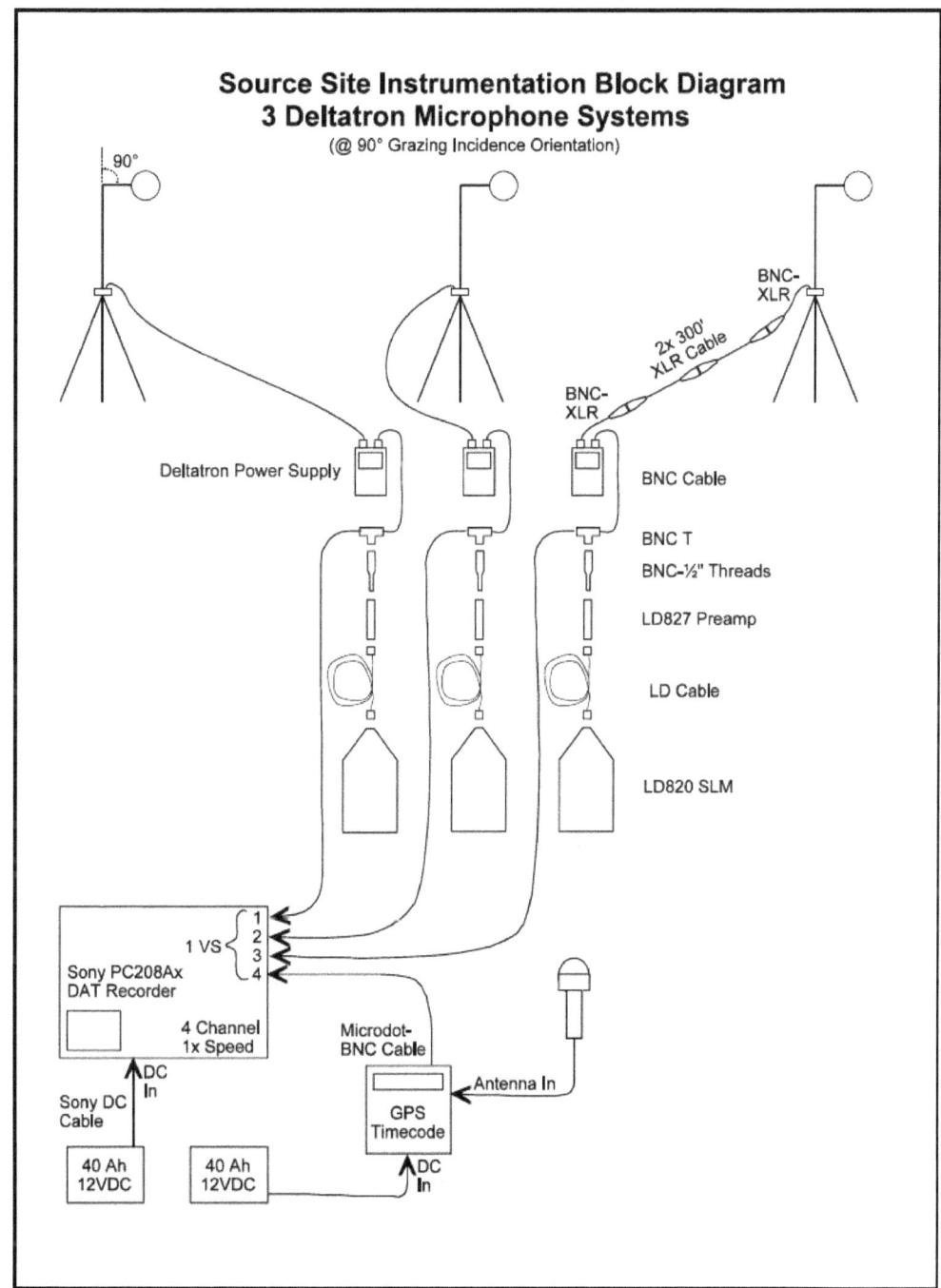

Figure 4. Block Diagram of Acoustic Instrumentation

2.3   Time-Space-Position Instrumentation

A digital video-based time-space-position-information (VTSPI) system was utilized to determine the position of tour aircraft overflights along an approximate 5 to 10 second segment of time in the vicinity of the Source Site. Four Canon Optura digital video cameras and four reference optical targets were deployed at known, fixed locations within the local coordinate system (see Figure 5). Two cameras were facing east-tracked helicopters; two cameras were facing west-tracked airplanes. Post-processing of the video data was performed using classic triangulation techniques to determine accurate time and position information for each aircraft event.

Figure 5. Digital Video-Based Time-Space-Position-Information System, Typical Setup

2.4   Ancillary Equipment

A differential global positioning system (dGPS) was utilized at the Source Site to establish the local coordinate system and precisely determine relative microphone, camera and target locations. The dGPS system consists primarily of two NovAtel Model RT20E GPS receivers, two GLB SNTR150 data link radios and an IBM 770 Thinkpad portable computer. Traditional surveying equipment was used for determining relative heights of the cameras and targets.

Meteorological data were collected at the Source Site utilizing Qualimetrics Transportable Automated Meteorological Systems (TAMS). The TAMS units collected average temperature, relative humidity, wind speed and direction, as well as barometric pressure, at five-minute intervals throughout the study.

TrueTime Model 705-305 GPS receiver/IRIG B timecode generators were used to precisely time-synchronize the video data, as well as all acoustic, meteorological and logging data at the Source Site.

3.   Data Reduction

This section discusses the development of the baseline acoustic data to be used as the reference database for the GCNP Noise Model Validation Study. Section 3.1 overviews the extensive quality control measures that were employed to ensure the highest quality source data. Section 3.2 discusses the data reduction process utilized in support of database development for NMSIM, INM and NODSS.

3.1   Data Culling

Quality control measures were established to ensure that the reference source data was of the highest possible quality. These measures included culling of events containing potentially contaminated acoustical data as well as events in which time-space-position data were potentially in question.

During the three-day measurement period, over 270 individual aircraft events were logged by the aircraft observer located at the Source Site. Based strictly on information included in the observer log, many of these events were immediately eliminated from the reference database. These eliminated aircraft events primarily included high altitude jets and GA aircraft not traveling along the Zuni Flight Corridor. Aircraft not positively identified were also eliminated. For example, a propeller aircraft may have been seen or heard, but the particular model may not have been positively identified.

The next step in the acoustic culling process was to manually examine the sound level time history data measured on-line at the Source Site. The sound level time history data measured by the LD820 at the source-site centerline microphone were used in concert with the aircraft observer log to identify potential acoustically "clean" events. Events with a minimum 15 dB uncontaminated rise and fall in the A-weighted time history and a time-correlated positive ID on the aircraft observer log were considered to be clean. Most clean aircraft events had a rise and fall in the A-weighted sound level time history of at least 15 dB and more often 20 to 40 dB. A large number of events had to be culled due to their close spacing (in time) with other events. For these culled events, the sound level associated with the first event did not significantly decrease prior to the increase in sound level associated with the second event. Figure 6 presents a typical A-weighted sound level time history of a designated clean event. As a result of the culling process, a total of 69 events were identified as potential acoustically clean events.

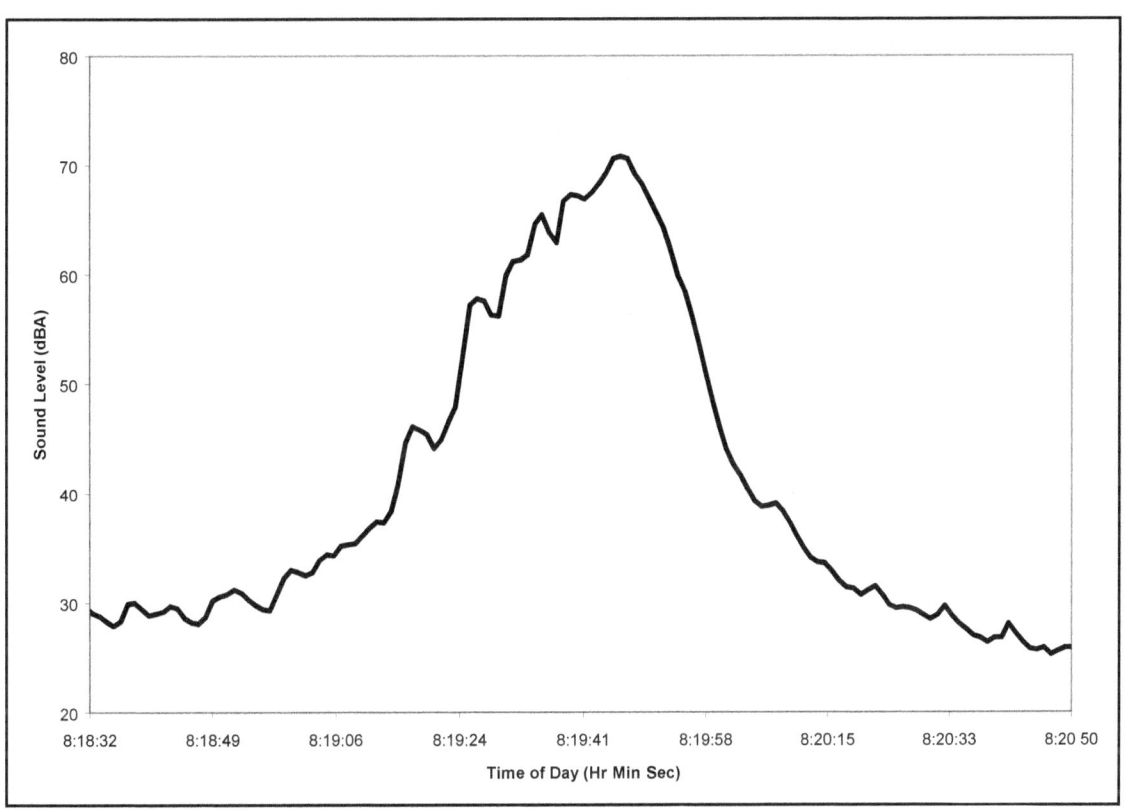

**Figure 6. Example of a Clean A-weighted Sound Level Time History,
Event 7: B206L, 9/12/99**

The next step in the culling process resulted from the acquisition of TSPI data for the 69 events. Many of the helicopter events and a few of the propeller events were so distant relative to the position of the video cameras that aircraft either could not be tracked with any degree of certainty, or in a few cases the aircraft could not be positively identified. Also, several of the helicopters were shielded from the cameras by local terrain features. As a result of the TSPI culling process, 28 events were identified as potentially clean events.

At this point in the culling process it is most appropriate to speak in terms of microphone events for the 3-microphone array. For example, 28 potentially clean events measured at three microphones translates into 84 possible microphone events.

The 84 microphone events identified as potentially clean events were then subjected to a more rigorous acoustic assessment. Specifically, the digital audio tape (DAT) recordings of each event at each of the three microphones were scrutinized for potential contamination. Any event with noticeable contamination of any kind (e.g. bird chirps or human activity) was eliminated. In addition to audio observations, the signal from the DAT was analyzed using a Hewlett Packard Model 35665a one-third octave-band analyzer. A time-history of sequential, half-second, linear data records was stored for each microphone event. The stored data for each event included the sound pressure level (SPL) for each one-third octave-band with a nominal center frequency between 50 Hz and 10 kHz. Once processed through the analyzer, any microphone event which did not meet a strict 10 dB rise and fall criterion was also eliminated.[1] Additionally, uncertainties in the aircraft position will effect noise levels as a function of $20\log(\Delta$slant-distance/slant-distance). To eliminate the corresponding uncertainty in noise levels, microphone events for the microphone *closest* to each aircraft flyover were eliminated. The final steps in the culling process yielded 39 total microphone events. These 39 events were used for the development of the reference database. The distribution of the 39 microphone events according to aircraft type was as follows: 4-AS350s; 1-B206B[2]; 8-B206Ls; 13-C207s; and 13-DHC-6s. Table 1 presents a summary of the 39 microphone events which were used in the development of the reference database.

3.2   Reference Acoustic Data

The linearly-averaged spectral time history data from the 39 microphone events were processed in a manner consistent with the procedures in the Federal Aviation Regulations (FAR) Part 36, *Noise Standards: Aircraft Type and Airworthiness Certification.* As-measured processing was performed, including sound level calibrations, system frequency response corrections and a fixed 7-dB per one-third octave-band sloping of all masked high-frequency data. In addition, simulated slow-scale averaging was performed in the processing using the equation for the continuous exponential as required by FAR Part 36. The net result of this process was deemed the as-measured corrected data.

---

[1]   Note that this 10 dB rise-and-fall criterion was based on the processed tape-recorded data for each individual microphone, whereas previously the 15 dB criterion was based on the data measured on-line by the SLM at the centerline microphone only.

[2]   Even though there was only 1 microphone event represented by the B206B, it was maintained as a separate entity from the B206L data because of a noticeably different spectral shape.

Table 1. Summary of 39 Microphone Events Utilized in Development of Reference Database

DATE	EVENT ID	A/C Type	Center Mic	East Mic	West Mic
09/10/1999	62	AS350			X
09/12/1999	34	AS350		X	
09/12/1999	59	AS350		X	
09/13/1999	86	B206B	X		
09/10/1999	28	B206L	X		X
09/10/1999	54	B206L	X		X
09/10/1999	79	B206L	X		X
09/12/1999	7	B206L	X		
09/13/1999	85	B206L	X		
09/10/1999	31	C207	X		
09/12/1999	18	C207	X	X	
09/12/1999	45	C207	X		
09/12/1999	46	C207	X	X	
09/12/1999	95	C207	X		
09/12/1999	97	C207	X		
09/13/1999	9	C207	X	X	
09/13/1999	10	C207	X	X	
09/13/1999	72	C207	X		
09/10/1999	59	DH6	X	X	
09/10/1999	60	DH6	X	X	
09/12/1999	26	DH6	X	X	
09/12/1999	44	DH6	X	X	
09/13/1999	14	DH6	X		
09/13/1999	16	DH6	X	X	
09/13/1999	80	DH6	X		
09/13/1999	81	DH6	X		

3.2.1 NMSIM Reference Spectral Time History Data

No further processing of the as-measured corrected data was required for input to NMSIM. NMSIM will utilize the slow-scale-averaged spectral time history data for the 39 microphone events, along with the associated TSPI data, and other event information included in the reference data spreadsheet which is outlined in Appendix A, and included with this letter report. Appendix B, Figures B-1 through B-5 present example spectral time history data for each of the 5 aircraft types represented. No attempt was made to average these spectral time history data since this would in effect confound the sound level versus emission angle relationship which is integral to NMSIM.

3.2.2   INM Reference Noise-Distance Data

A substantial amount of additional processing of these data was necessary to generate noise versus distance (N-D) values for input to the Integrated Noise Model (INM). The process utilized was consistent with the simplified correction procedure identified in FAR Part 36 as well as in SAE-AIR-1845. For each of the 39 microphone events, the test-day maximum A-weighted sound level (MXSA, denoted by the symbol L_{ASmx}), the as-measured, corrected, test-day spectrum obtained at the time of L_{ASmx}, the sound exposure level (SEL, denoted by the symbol L_{AE}), and the test-day distance at closest-point-of-approach to the aircraft were identified. These data were then used in a two-step correction process to generate an N-D curve for each microphone event. As part of this two step process, the as-measured, corrected, test-day spectrum is effectively corrected to the source aircraft (Step 1), and then to the ten INM reference distances of 200, 400, 630, 1000, 2000, 4000, 6300 10000, 16000, and 25000 ft (Step 2). For generating the reference L_{AE} N-D curve, the correction process takes into account divergence, distance duration, the effects of off-reference aircraft speed and atmospheric absorption. For generating the reference L_{ASmx} N-D curve, the correction process accounts for divergence and atmospheric absorption. The distance duration correction and the velocity correction are not applied since the spectrum at the time of maximum sound level is independent of aircraft speed and the duration of the event. Corrections to be applied to the test-day L_{AE} and L_{ASmx} values are based on the following general equation, where the second and third terms do not apply for L_{ASmx}:

$$\Delta L = 20\log(d_{test}/d_{ref}) + 10\log(d_{ref}/d_{test}) + 10\log(v_{test}/v_{ref}) + \Delta L_{atm}$$

where: ΔL is the correction to be applied to the test-day L_{AE} or L_{ASmx} (dB);
d_{test} is the test-day distance at closest-point-of-approach to the aircraft (ft);
d_{ref} is the reference-day INM distance of 200, 400, 630, 1000, 2000, 4000, 6300, 10000, 16000 or 25000 (ft);
v_{test} is the test-day aircraft speed (kts);
v_{ref} is the reference-day aircraft speed, which is 160 for INM (kts); and

ΔL_{atm} is the atmospheric absorption correction computed using the equations of SAE-ARP-866a, assuming test-day temperature and relative humidity conditions as measured at the Source Site, and assuming a reference-day temperature of 71.4 degrees F and relative humidity of 38.1 percent.[3]

Figures 7 and 8 present the N-D relationships for each of the five aircraft types for the L_{AE} and the L_{ASmx}, respectively. These curves represent the energy-averaged N-D curve taking into account the 39 microphone events. Table 2 presents a summary of the noise data plotted in these curves. Appendix C, Figures C-1 through C-10 present the individual N-D curves for each of the 39 microphone events, along with the energy-averaged curves shown in Figures 7 and 8.

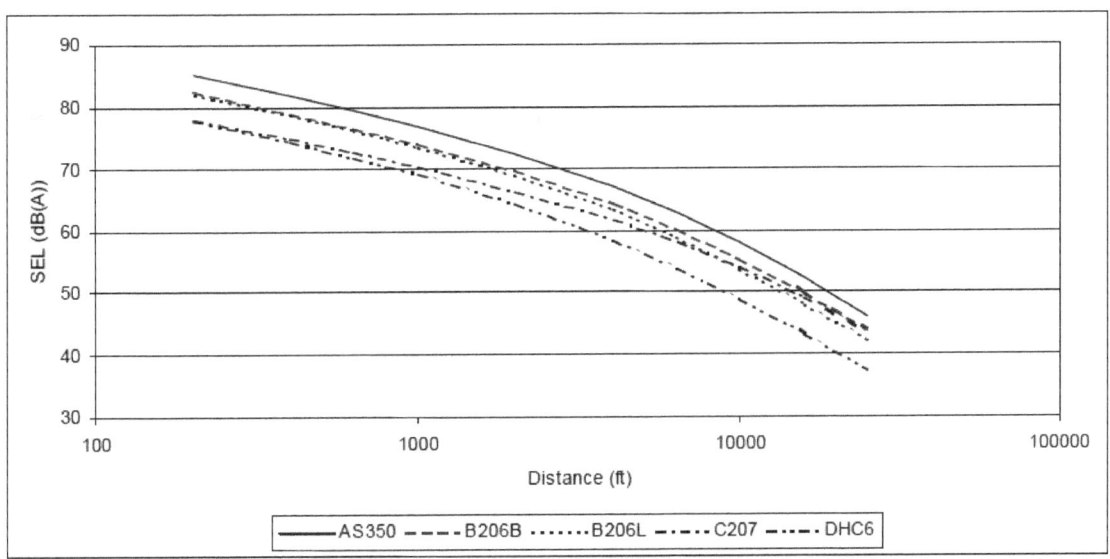

**Figure 7. Reference L_{AE}-Versus-Distance Curves for INM
Corrected to 160 kts at 71.4 degrees F and 38.1 Percent RH**

---

[3]   For each event, temperatures and relative humidity data were taken from the Source Site meteorological station from the 5-minute sample that was closest to the time of maximum A-weighted sound level. Some data on September 12 (Events 18, 26, 95 and 97) were taken from the Grandview meteorological station, due to lack of data at the Source Site. Reference day conditions (71.4 degrees F and 38.1 percent relative humidity) were determined by algebraically averaging the meteorological conditions associated with the clean events.

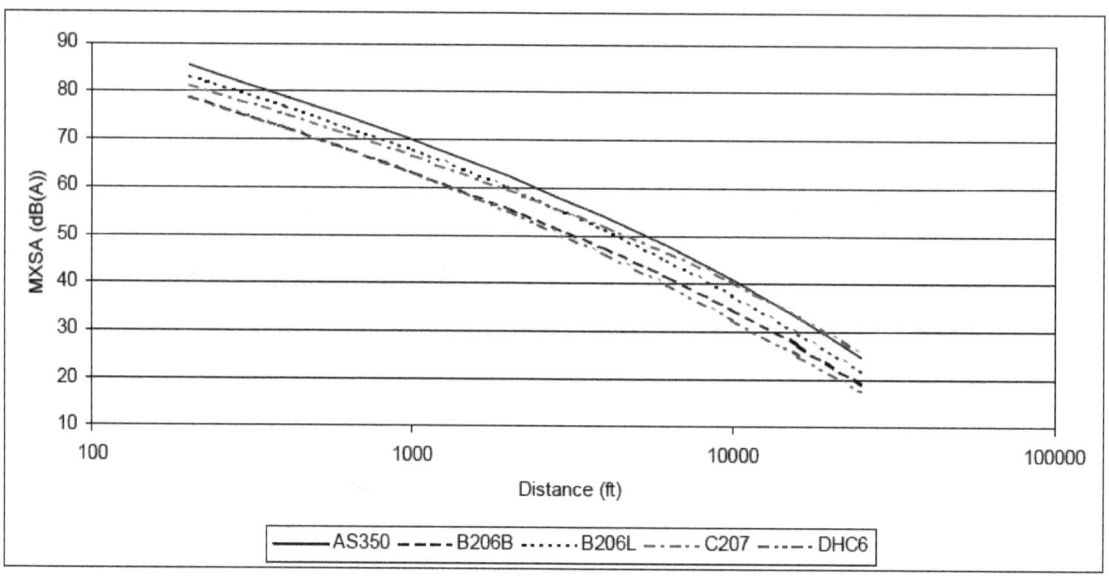

**Figure 8. Reference L$_{ASmx}$-Versus-Distance Curves for INM
Corrected to 71.4 degrees F and 38.1 Percent RH**

Sensitivity analyses were also conducted to determine if the measured data were dependent upon either source-to-receptor elevation angle or aircraft test speed. Note that cursory analysis did not indicate a dependence on aircraft operator. Figure 9 presents the reference L$_{AE}$ data (corrected to 1000 ft and 160 kts) as a function of elevation angle. Simple linear regressions are plotted through these data for each of the five aircraft types. Because the data are generally clustered in a relatively small range of elevation angles between 5 and 30 degrees, a statistical analysis of the slope of the regression line is probably not appropriate. However, there does not appear to be a dependence of the measured data on elevation angle for the range of angles represented.

Figure 10 presents the reference L$_{AE}$ data (corrected to 1000 ft and 160 kts) as a function of the original test speed for that event. Since the L$_{AE}$ data are all corrected to a reference speed of 160 kts, any effect could be considered a residual effect of speed on the reference source level, i.e., a source noise effect. It was thought that this may be an issue with helicopters in particular, since their noise levels have been shown to closely correlate with blade-tip-mach-number, which is directly associated with speed. Although one could argue that there may be a slight effect, especially for the B206L, there is not enough data to make any type of meaningful correction for source noise. Further, since all of the data are averaged together, a correction is probably unnecessary.

Table 2. Summary of Reference Noise-Versus-Distance Relationships Corrected to 71.4 degrees F and 38.1 Percent RH, and 160 kts for L_{AE}

Distance (ft)	AIRCRAFT									
	AS350		B206B		B206L		C207		DHC-6	
	L_{AE}	L_{ASmx}	L_{AE}	L_{ASmx}	L_{AE}	L_{ASmx}	L_{AE}	L_{ASmx}	L_{AE}	L_{ASmx}
200	85.2	85.4	82.5	78.8	82.1	83.4	78.1	81.5	77.9	79.0
400	81.8	79.0	79.1	72.4	78.7	77.0	74.9	75.3	74.4	72.4
630	79.4	74.6	76.7	68.0	76.3	72.6	72.7	71.1	71.9	68.0
1000	76.8	70.0	74.1	63.4	73.6	67.9	70.3	66.7	69.1	63.2
2000	72.4	62.5	69.6	55.9	69.0	60.3	66.4	59.8	64.3	55.3
4000	67.0	54.1	64.3	47.6	63.4	51.6	61.8	52.2	58.5	46.4
6300	62.8	47.9	60.2	41.5	58.9	45.1	58.3	46.7	54.0	39.9
10000	58.0	40.9	55.5	34.7	53.7	37.7	54.1	40.5	48.8	32.7
16000	52.2	33.0	49.9	27.1	47.9	29.6	49.1	33.3	43.1	25.1
25000	46.0	24.8	43.8	19.1	42.2	21.7	43.5	25.7	37.5	17.8

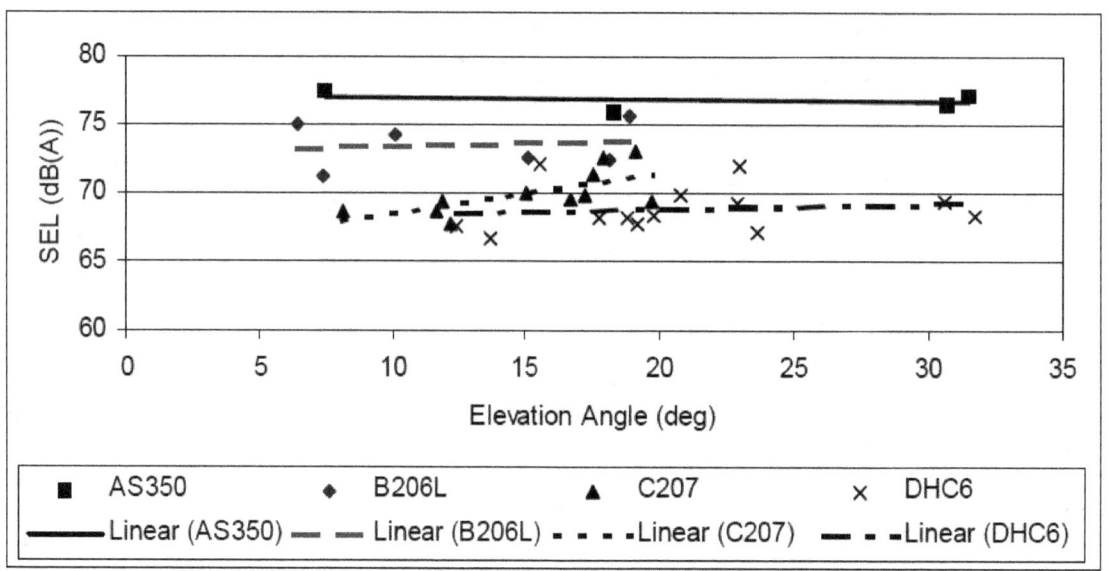

Figure 9. Reference L_{AE} Versus Elevation Angle, Corrected to 1000 ft and 160 kts

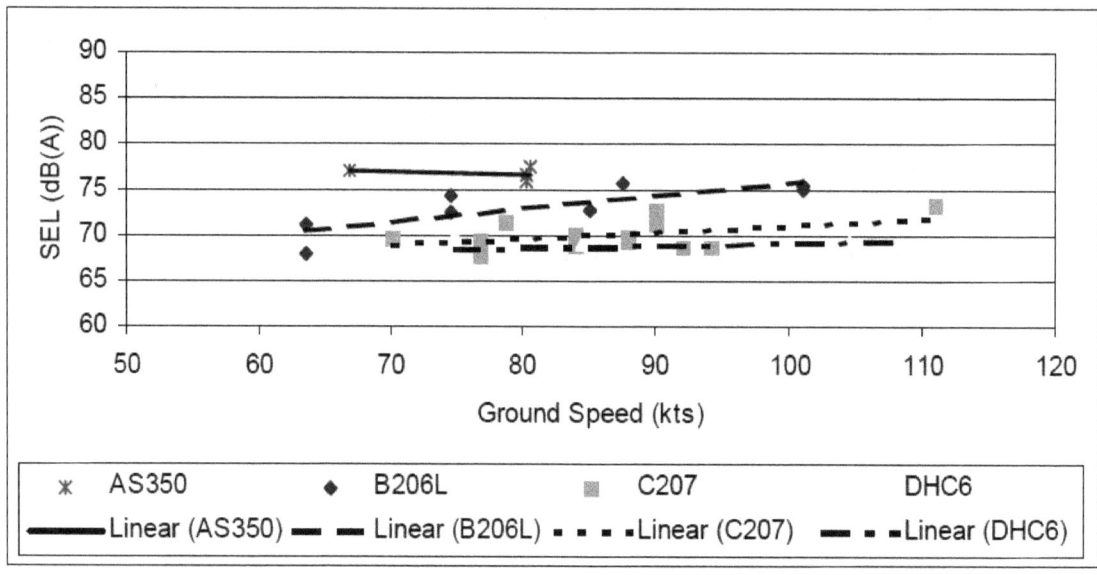

Figure 10. Reference L_{AE} Versus Test Speed, Corrected to 1000 ft and 160 kts

3.2.3   NODSS Reference Spectral Data

The required reference source data for NODSS is effectively a subset of that required for the INM. Specifically, NODSS requires a single spectrum for each aircraft type corrected to a reference atmospheric condition at a distance of 1000 ft at the time of maximum A-weighted sound level. To satisfy this requirement, the same two-step correction process used to develop INM N-D curves was used to develop reference spectra for NODSS. For each of the 39 microphone events, the as-measured, corrected, test-day spectrum obtained at the time of L_{ASmx}, and the test-day distance at closest-point-of-approach to the aircraft were identified. As was the case when generating the INM L_{ASmx} N-D curve, the correction process only takes into account divergence and atmospheric absorption (reference day temperature and relative humidity of 71.4 degrees F and 38.1 percent, respectively). Figure 11 presents the corrected spectra for each of the five aircraft types. These spectra are the energy-averaged spectra for all of the microphone events for a particular aircraft type. Table 3 presents a summary of the energy-averaged spectral data. In addition, Appendix D, Figures D-1 through D-5 present, for each aircraft type, respectively, the individual spectra which make up the energy-averaged spectra shown in Figure 11.

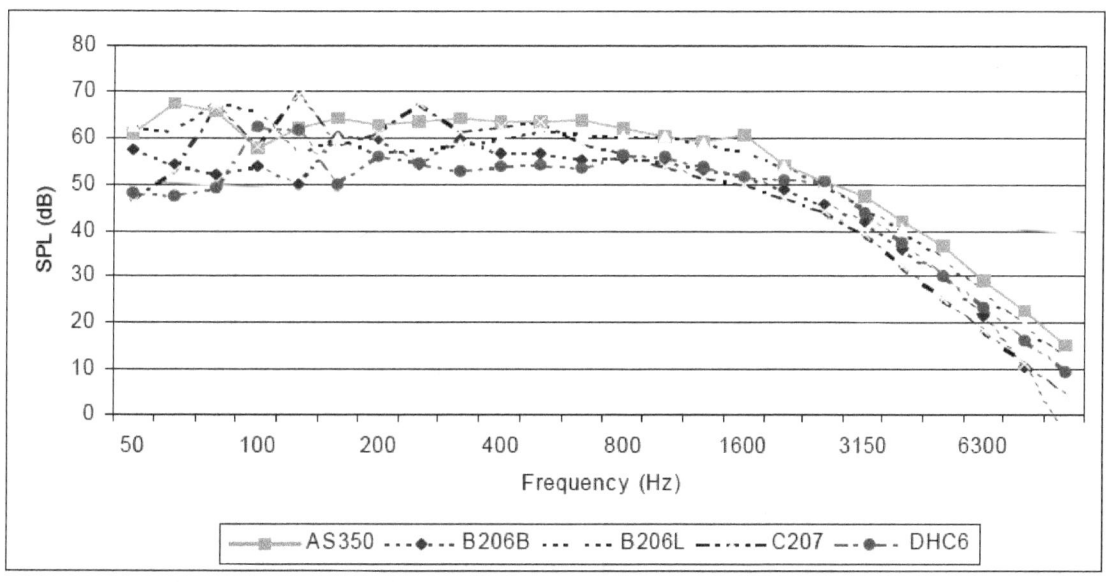

Figure 11. Reference Spectra for NODSS
Corrected to 1000 ft at 71.4 degrees F and 38.1 Percent RH

Table 3. Summary of Reference Energy-Averaged Spectra
Corrected to 1000 ft at 71.4 degrees F and 38.1 Percent RH

Frequency (Hz)	AIRCRAFT				
	AS350	B206B	B206L	C207	DHC-6
50	60.9	57.5	62.4	46.3	48.1
63	67.5	54.1	61.2	52.8	47.4
80	65.7	51.9	67.7	66.8	49.2
100	57.7	53.7	65.6	57.9	62.6
125	62.2	49.8	56.7	69.3	61.6
160	64.1	60.4	59.8	58.6	50.0
200	62.9	59.9	56.7	61.0	56.0
250	63.6	54.3	57.5	67.6	54.4
315	64.1	59.9	58.5	61.4	52.8
400	63.6	56.7	59.8	62.4	53.9
500	63.4	56.6	61.2	63.7	54.2
630	63.9	55.2	61.1	58.7	53.5
800	62.1	55.5	60.4	56.7	56.4
1000	60.2	54.8	60.3	53.8	55.9
1250	59.3	53.1	58.8	51.2	53.7
1600	60.6	51.8	57.0	49.9	51.6
2000	54.2	48.8	53.9	47.1	50.8
2500	50.7	45.5	49.8	44.0	50.4
3150	47.3	42.0	44.9	39.1	43.9
4000	41.8	36.0	40.3	32.2	37.2
5000	36.6	30.2	33.7	25.2	30.2
6300	29.0	21.7	26.4	18.2	23.2
8000	22.6	10.4	19.3	11.2	16.2
10000	15.1	-4.7	12.3	-4.3	9.2

4.   Speed Data Reduction

Aircraft speeds were calculated for a total of 104 events, representing six types of aircraft flying along the Zuni Corridor. A series of four reference points were used to determine aircraft speeds along the Corridor. Three of the reference points, along with a projection to the fourth, are shown in Figure 12, with their specific locations summarized in Table 4. At the first reference location, the Source Site centerline microphone, aircraft were initially identified for speed calculations based on the aircraft observer logs maintained at the site. Time-of-day (TOD) information for each aircraft event was determined using the TOD associated with the on-line L_{ASmx} measured at the Source Site centerline microphone (T_1). Aircraft type and TOD data were also collected at the second reference location, the Cape Final Site (T_2). As depicted in Figure 13 below, a unique topographical feature, Gold Hill, was used by the aircraft observer to consistently note the time of aircraft passing the Cape Final Site, headed north in the corridor. The location of Gold Hill was verified at the TopoZone web site (http://www.topozone.com) based on a recommendation by the NPS. The flight time, T_{FLIGHT} (T_2 - T_1), was then calculated for corresponding aircraft events identified at the two sites.

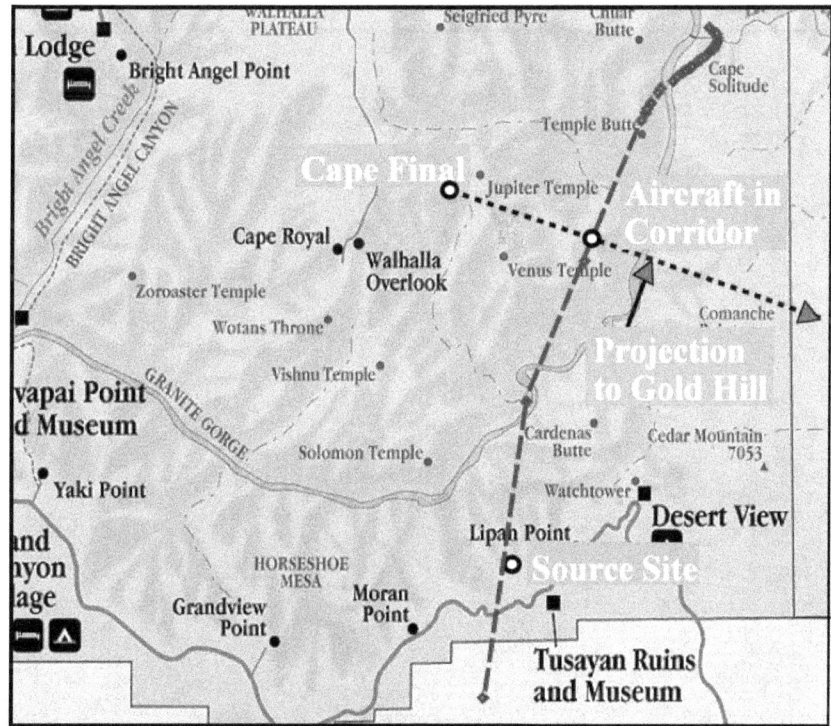

Figure 12. Reference Points for Aircraft Speed Computations

Table 4. Summary of Reference Points for Aircraft Speed Computations

Location #	Location	Latitude (degrees)	Longitude (degrees)
1	Source Site	36.02366	-111.88266
2	Cape Final	36.14639	-111.90972
3	Gold Hill	36.1111	-111.7422
4	Approximate Aircraft Location in Zuni Corridor	36.12487	-111.84826

Figure 13. View of Aircraft and Gold Hill from Cape Final Site

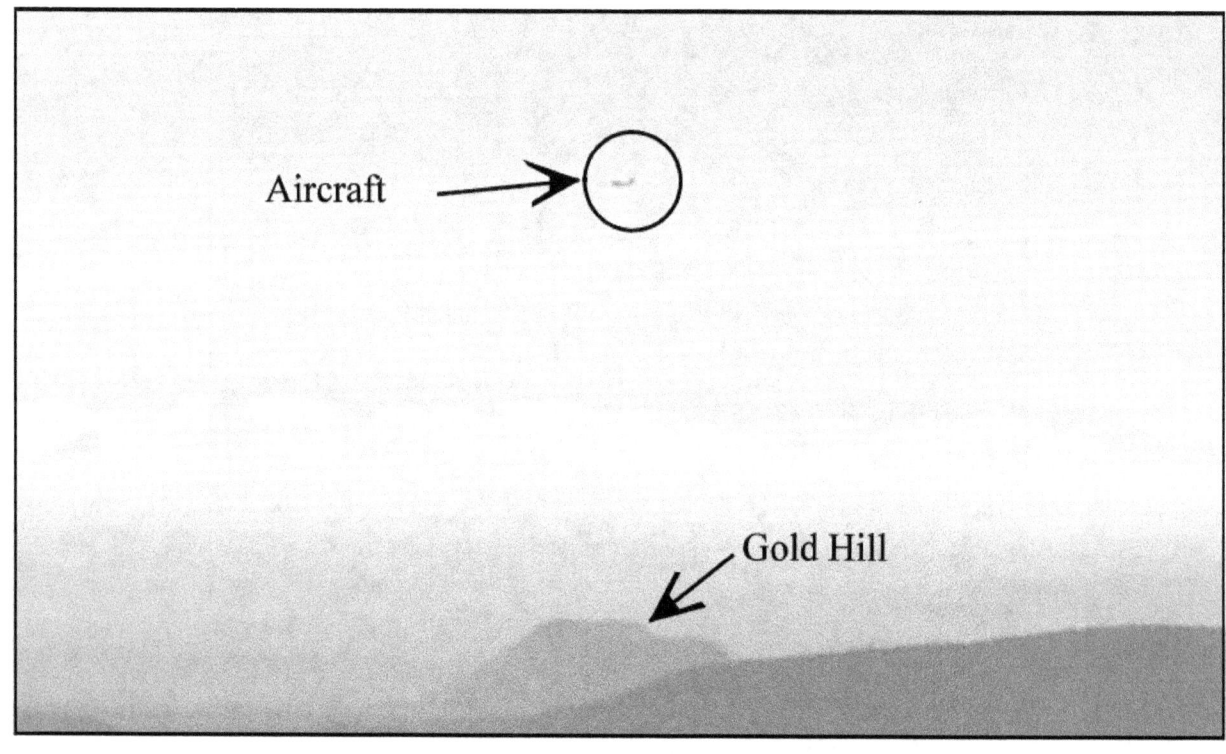

For the calculation of speed, the distance along the Zuni Flight Corridor associated with T_{FLIGHT} had to be determined. The first step in this process was to determine the approximate location of the aircraft along the Zuni Flight Corridor when they were identified by the observer stationed at Cape Final. This was determined by estimating the intersection of the flight corridor and a projection defined by the observer location and the topographic feature. The intersection point is also displayed in Figure 12.

Given the relative position of both the Source Site and the identified aircraft position along the corridor, the distance the aircraft traveled [D] was calculated to be approximately 41,000 feet, or 8 miles. Given D, individual aircraft speeds were then calculated as follows:

$$V_{AC} \text{ [kts]} = \{D \text{ [ft]} / T_{FLIGHT} \text{ [min]}\} \times 60 \text{ [min/hr]} \times 1/5280 \text{ [mile/ft]} \times 0.8684 \text{ [kts/mi]}$$

A summary of the average speed data for each aircraft type is presented in Table 5.[4]

Table 5. Summary of Average Speed Data

Aircraft	# of Events	Average Speed (kts)	Std. Dev. (kts)
AS350	9	87	6.3
B206B	6	100	0.8
B206L	26	94	4.7
C207	23	115	5.9
DHC-6	19	104	4.6

A comparison was made of the aircraft speed data and that calculated using the VTSPI system at the Source Site for individual events. As expected, the aircraft speeds were either extremely close or slightly higher than those measured at the Source Site. Given that the aircraft are just entering the Zuni Corridor in the proximity of the Source Site, it does not seem unreasonable to assume that they

---

[4]   Note that the total number of events displayed in the table is 83, rather than 104. Averages and standard deviations were initially computed for the 104 events processed. Subsequently, all events with speeds larger than two standard deviations from the average speed for a particular aircraft type were discarded. Additionally, only one Cessna 210 event was available for speed calculations; this is not presented for comparative purposes.

accelerate to slightly higher speeds further along in the corridor. For the three helicopters (AS350, B206B and B206L) the comparable speeds were generally within 10 kts. For the C207 aircraft the comparable speeds were on average 16 kts faster than was measured at the Source Site. Comparable differences for the DeHavilland DHC-6 appeared to be less uniform than for the other aircraft, but were generally within 15 kts.

5.   Comparison of Noise-Versus-Distance Data

This section presents a comparison of the INM reference noise-versus-distance data presented in Section 3.2.2 with that used in previous GCNP noise modeling efforts documented in the February 2000 Final Supplemental Environmental Assessment for GCNP. Figures 14 through 18 present the differences between the L_{AE} versus distance data developed as part of the current effort and that used in the previous GCNP modeling effort.[5] A positive difference indicates that levels developed in the current study are lower than those used in previous studies. As can be seen, all difference values are positive. Differences for the AS350 range from 0.9 to 4.6 dB. Differences for the B206B range from 2.2 to 5.2 dB. Differences for the B206L range from 3.5 to 6.8 dB.[6] Differences for the C207 range from 6.0 to 9.3 dB. Differences for the DHC-6 range from 2.2 to 5.3 dB. This consistently positive difference indicates that the aircraft operating in GCNP are actually lower in level compared with reference sound levels used in previous analysis. This is an important observation in that it indicates that previous modeling efforts utilized conservative source noise levels with regard to assessing impacts.

---

[5]   Note that the L_{AE} versus distance data used in the previous GCNP modeling effort included an acoustic impedance adjustment of -1.1 dB. This adjustment, which is typically computed and applied directly by the INM, was assumed to be inherent in the measured data. The computed adjustment was based on an altitude of 7000 ft and a temperature of 71.4 degrees F.

[6]   For the three helicopters, the L_{AE} versus distance data used in the previous GCNP modeling efforts, although adapted for use in INM, originated from the database of the FAA's Heliport Noise Model, which only includes L_{AE} data to a distance of 10000 ft. Since INM requires data to distances of 16000 and 25000 ft, these data were derived previously through extrapolation of the L_{AE} data at 6300 and 10000 ft. The L_{AE} data at 16000 and 25000 ft in the current analysis were computed using the more traditional methodologies over viewed in Section 3. It is clear from the data in Figures 14 through 16, that the empirical approach used previously to derive L_{AE} data at 16000 and 25000 ft introduced error as compared with the more traditional approach. This helps to explain the counterintuitive behavior in Figures 14 through 16 for distances larger than about 10000 ft.

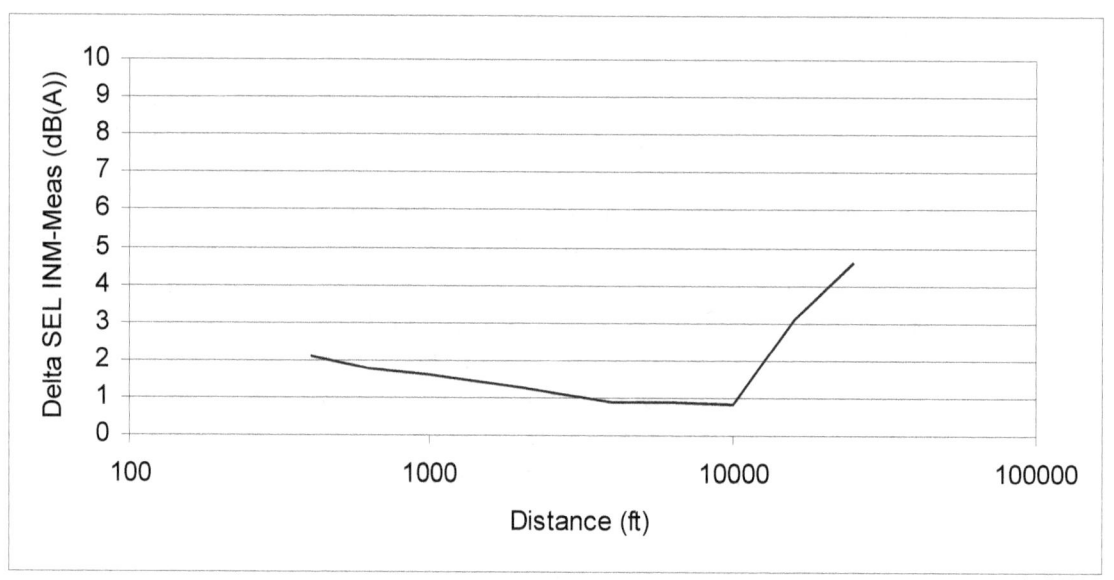

Figure 14. Difference in L$_{AE}$-Versus-Distance Data for AS350

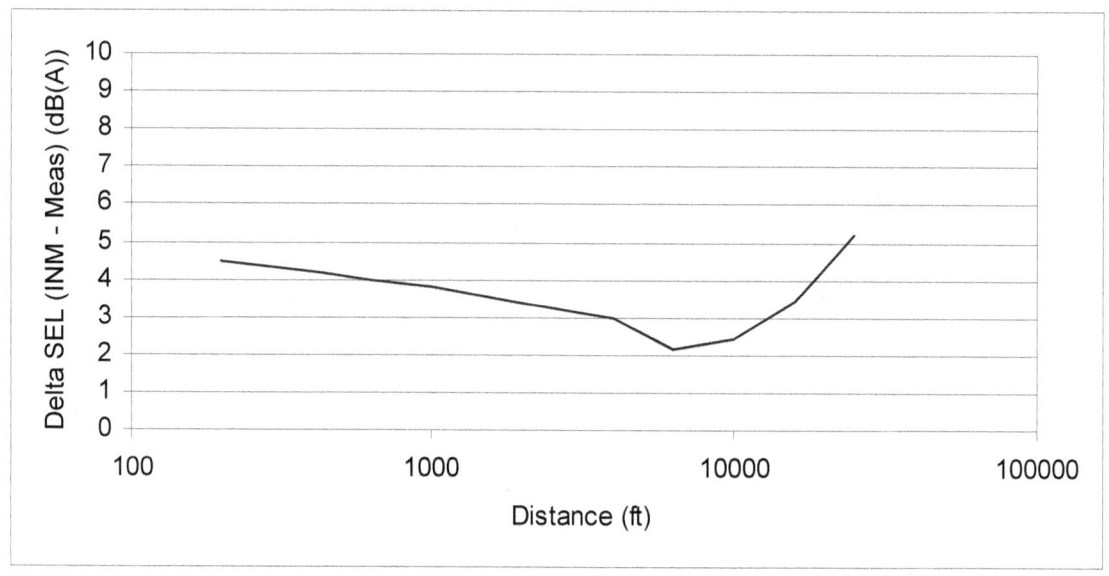

Figure 15. Difference in L$_{AE}$-Versus-Distance Data for B206B

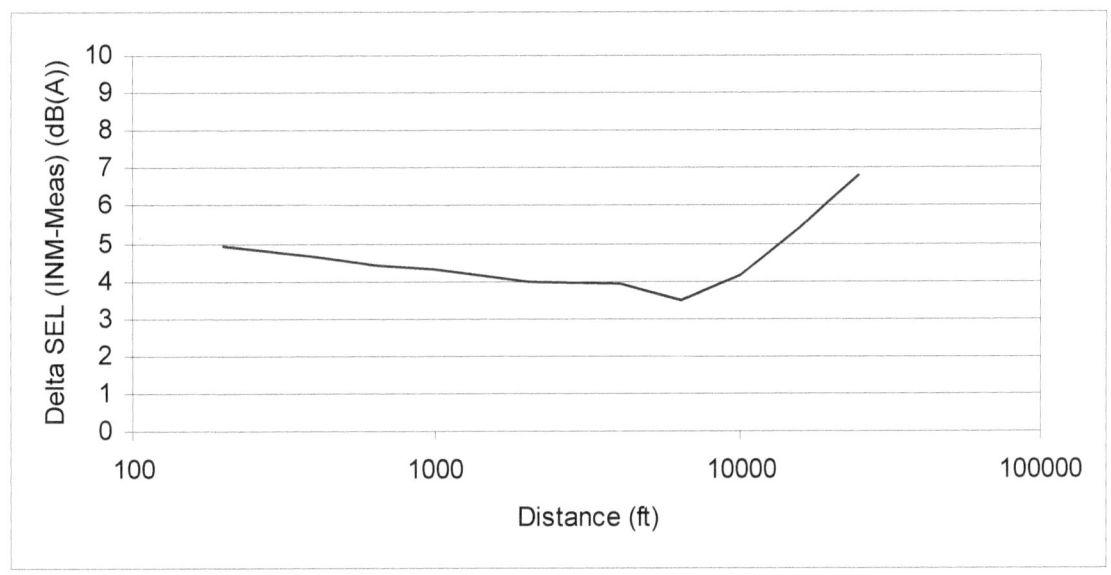

Figure 16. Difference in L$_{AE}$-Versus-Distance Data for B206L

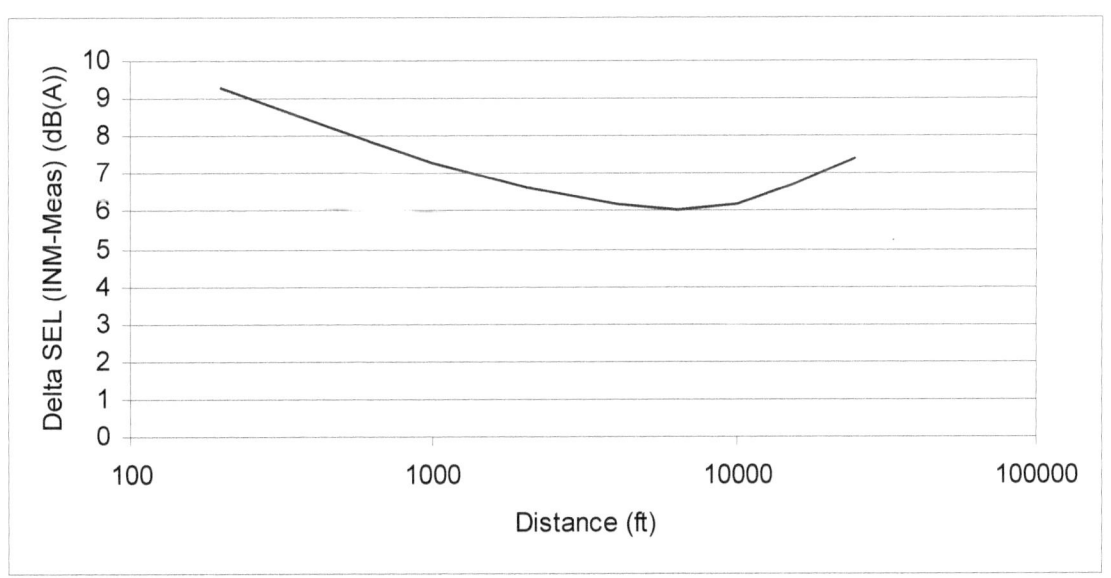

Figure 17. Difference in L$_{AE}$-Versus-Distance Data for C207

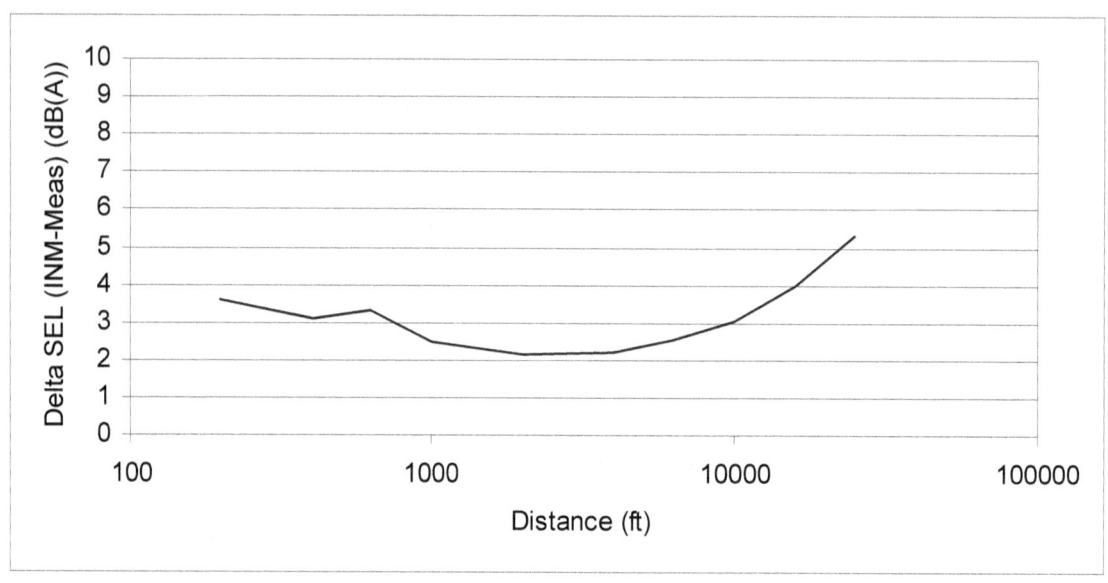

Figure 18. Difference in L$_{AE}$-Versus-Distance Data for DHC-6

Appendix A
Summary Spreadsheet for Reference Data

This appendix overviews the data contained within the summary spreadsheet used to develop the reference information required for input to the three computer models. The spreadsheet includes the entire set of observer-based aircraft event data logged at the Source Site during the GCNP noise model validation study. An electronic copy of the spreadsheet is included with this letter report. The variables included in the spreadsheet are as follows:
****
***** DATE: Date the aircraft event observations were made.
***** EVENT ID: A sequential aircraft event designator.
***** A/C Type: The specific type of aircraft observed, where:
*****   C207: Cessna Model 207 propeller airplane
*****   DH6: DeHavilland Model DHC-6 propeller airplane with quiet props
*****   B206L: Bell Model 206 Longranger helicopter
*****   B206B: Bell Model 206 Jetranger helicopter
*****   AS350: Aerospatiale Model AS350 helicopter
***** Operator: The commercial operator of the specific aircraft event observed, where:
*****   AGC: Air Grand Canyon
*****   PAP: Papilion Airlines
*****   GCA: Grand Canyon Airlines
*****   KEN: Kennai Helicopters
*****   ROCKY: Rocky Airlines
*****   AS: Airstar
***** Direction: South to North (N) up Zuni or North to South (S) Down Zuni.
***** OBS Start: Field observed aircraft event start time.
***** OBS End: Field observed aircraft event end time.
***** Overlap?: Used as a first cut to filter out potentially contaminated aircraft events for acoustic processing. Y means overlap, N means no
*****   overlap. N(1) means overlap times coincide at beginning or end of aircraft event. N(2) means times coincide at beginning and
*****   end of aircraft event.
***** Time @ Max: Time at maximum sound level from manual analysis of online SLM time history data at the centerline microphone.
***** Ground Speed: Ground Speed calculated from video tracking data
***** Temperature/RH : Temperature/RH at Source Site taken from nearest five minute sample. (Except: 9/12 #18, 26, 95, 97 where data was
*****   taken from met station at Grandview)
***** Video Track Regressions: Linear regression coefficients through video track data, where the X-Y regression would define the track
*****   through the microphone line (the XY intercept is the lateral offset when the AC passed the mic line) and the X-Z regression would
*****   define the altitude profile (the XZ intercept is the altitude of the AC when it passed the mic line)
***** The next group of columns contain the acoustic and AC position data on a per microphone basis
***** On-Line Max LEQ: This is the maximum 1 second LEQ for centerline microphone events processed in initial processing (center mic only).
***** As-Measured LAsmx: The ½ second, slow-scale response, maximum A-weighted sound level, corrected for calibration drift and system
*****   frequency response.
***** AS-Measured SEL: The sound exposure level over the 10 dB-down duration of the event.
***** Altitude: The altitude of the aircraft over the microphone
***** SR: The distance from the microphone to the aircraft.
***** Beta: The elevation angle of the aircraft
***** AC Side: The side of the aircraft (Left or Right) which was facing the microphone, relative to the direction of flight.
***** Sound Exposure Level vs. Distance: The sound exposure level corrected for spherical spreading, atmospheric absorption (reference day =
*****   71.4 deg F, 38.1% RH), speed (160 kts) and duration at each of 10 INM reference distances at each microphone.
***** Maximum A-weighted Level vs. Distance: The Maximum A-weighted sound level corrected for spherical spreading and atmospheric
*****   absorption at each of 10 INM reference distances at each microphone.
***** Spectrum Corrected to 1000 ft: The one-third octave-band sound pressure levels (50 Hz - 10000 Hz) corrected
*****   for spherical spreading and atmospheric absorption to a distance of 1000 ft. Note that bands identified as masked per FAR 36 are
*****   shaded red.

Appendix B
NMSIM Reference Spectral Time History Data

This appendix presents example reference spectral time history data for each of the 5 aircraft types represented. These data will be used as input data for NMSIM. Figures B-1 through B-5 present example spectral time history data for the AS350, B206B, B206L, C207 and DHC-6, respectively.

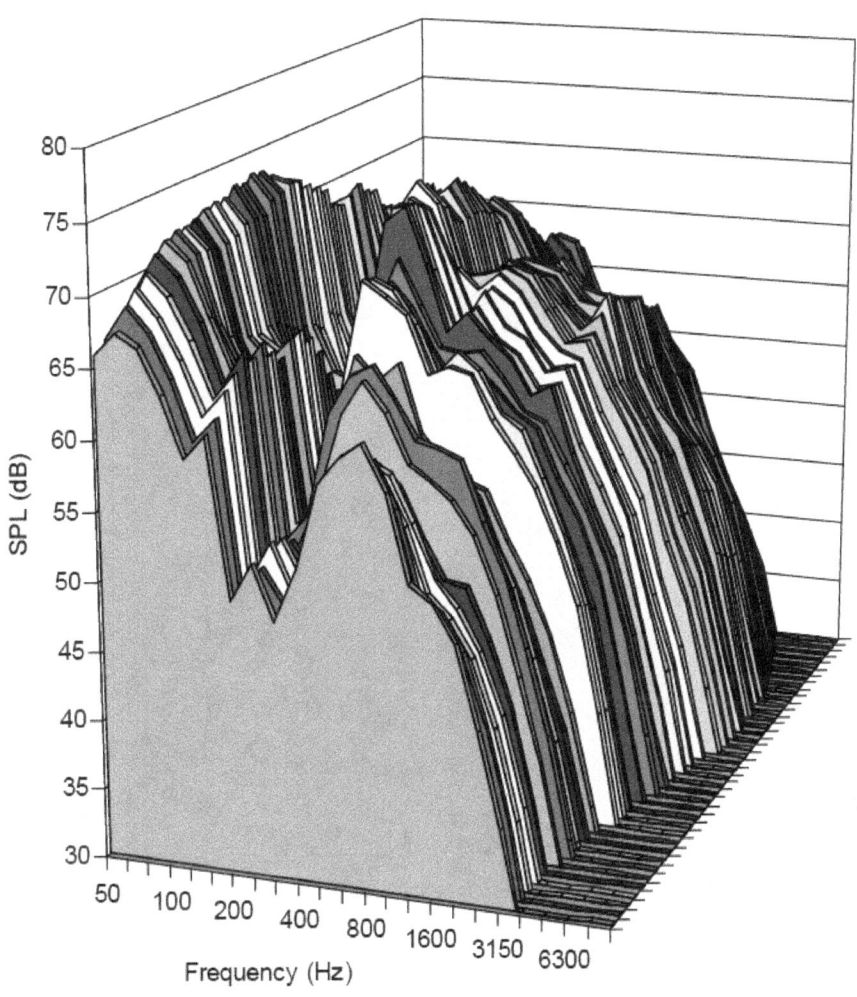

Figure B-1. Example Reference Spectral Time History for NMSIM, AS350

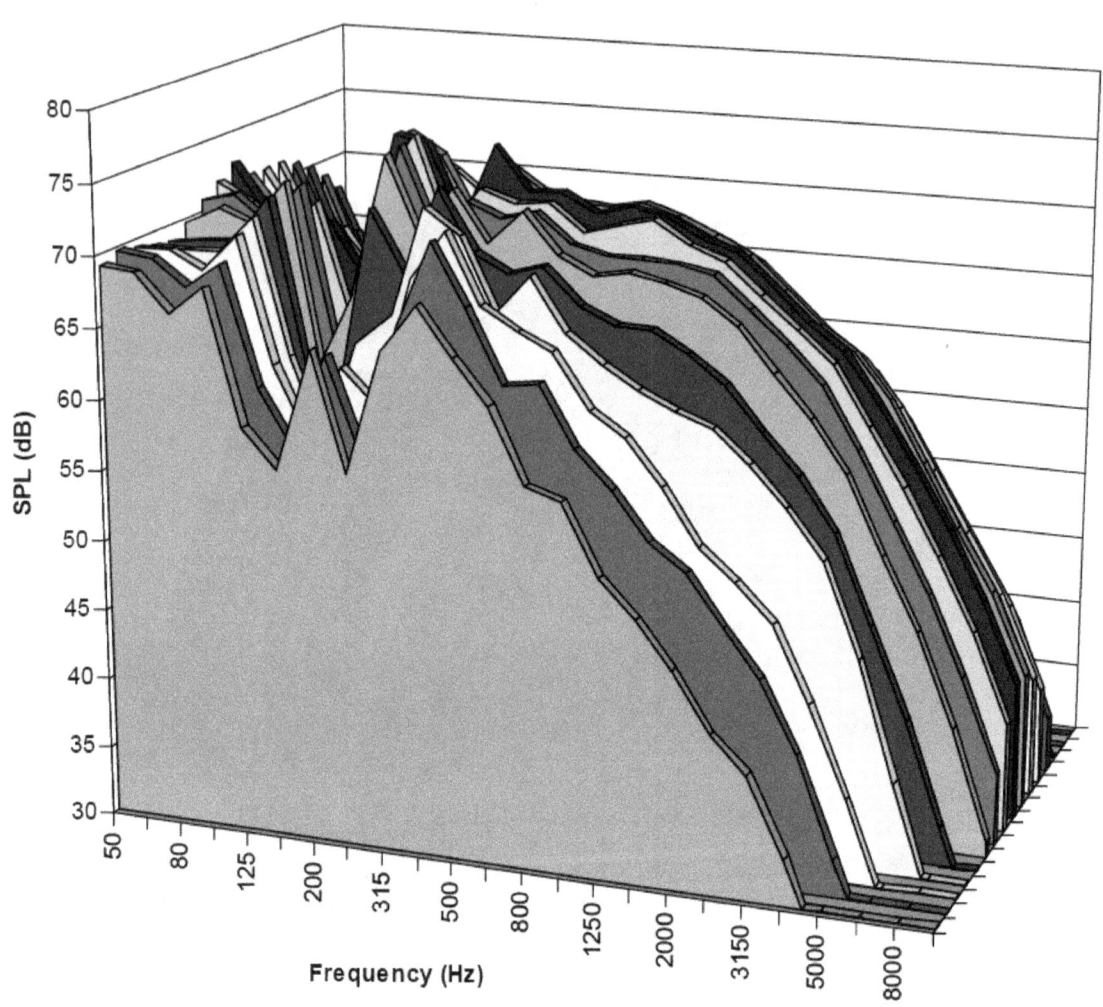

Figure B-2. Example Reference Spectral Time History for NMSIM, B206B

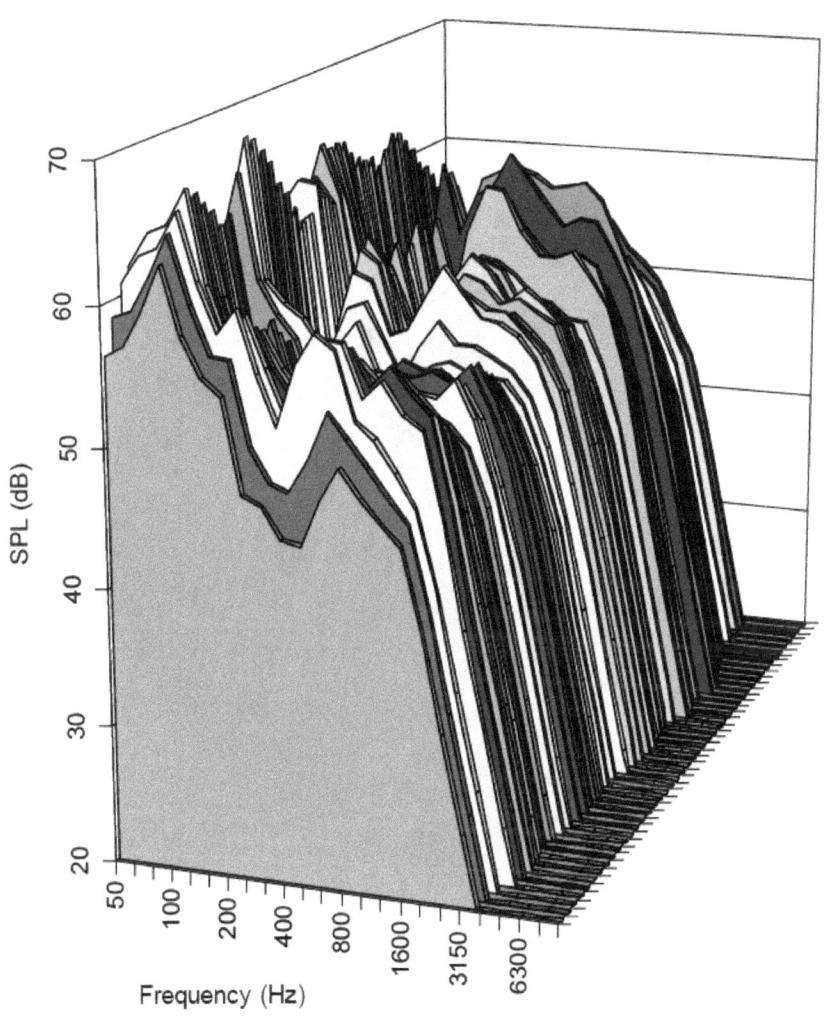

Figure B-3. Example Reference Spectral Time History for NMSIM, B206L

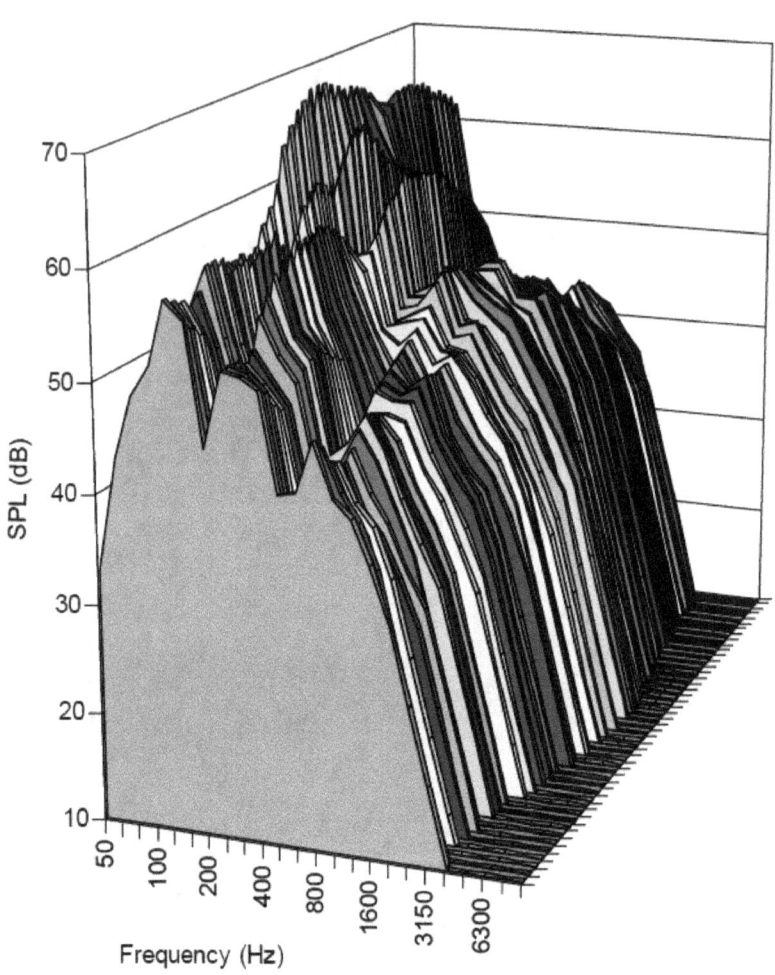

Figure B-4. Example Reference Spectral Time History for NMSIM, C207

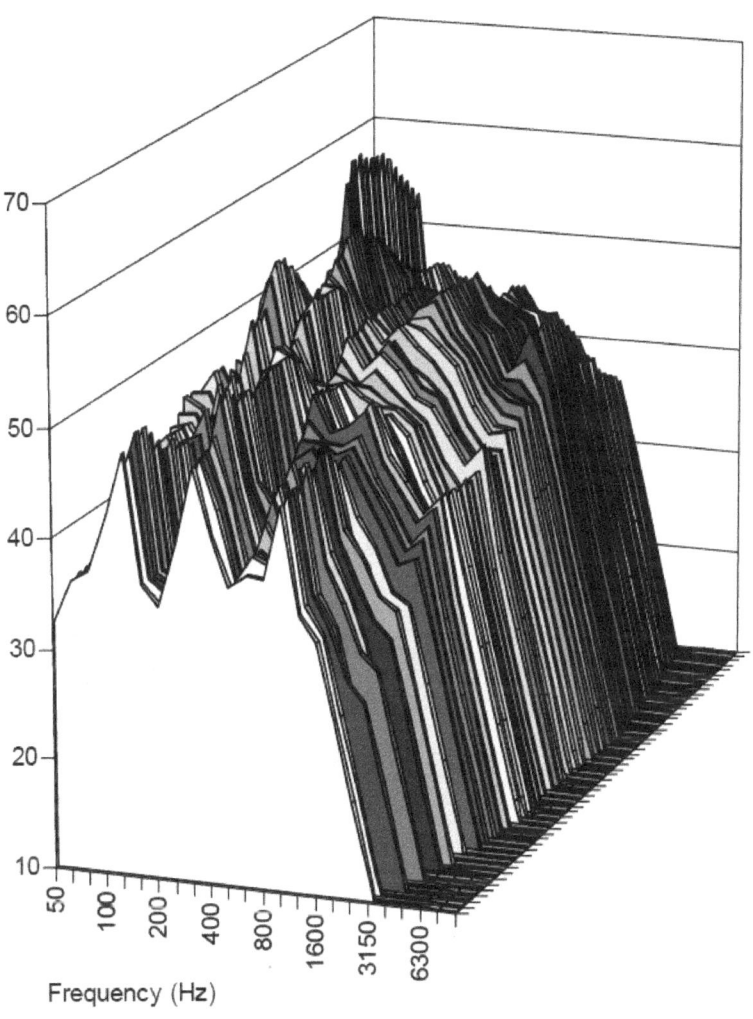

Figure B-5. Example Reference Spectral Time History for NMSIM, DHC-6

Appendix C
INM Noise-Distance Data

This appendix presents the individual N-D curves for the 39 microphone events, along with the associated energy-averaged curves. Figures C-1 through C-5 present the L_{AE} versus distance curves for the AS350, B206B, B206L, C207 and DHC-6, respectively. Figures C-6 through C-10 present the L_{ASmx} versus distance data for the AS350, B206B, B206L, C207 and DHC-6, respectively.

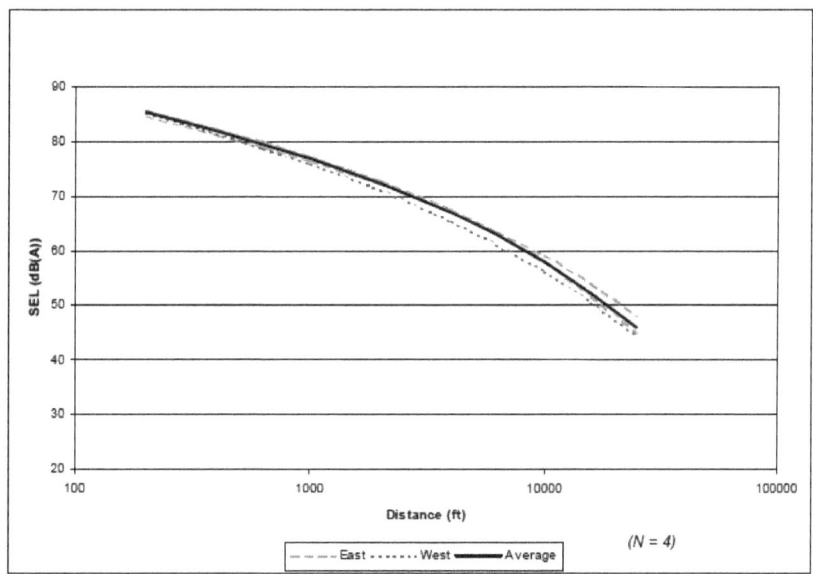

**Figure C-1. Reference L$_{AE}$-Versus-Distance Curves for INM, AS350,
Corrected to 160 kts at 71.4 degrees F and 38.1 Percent RH**

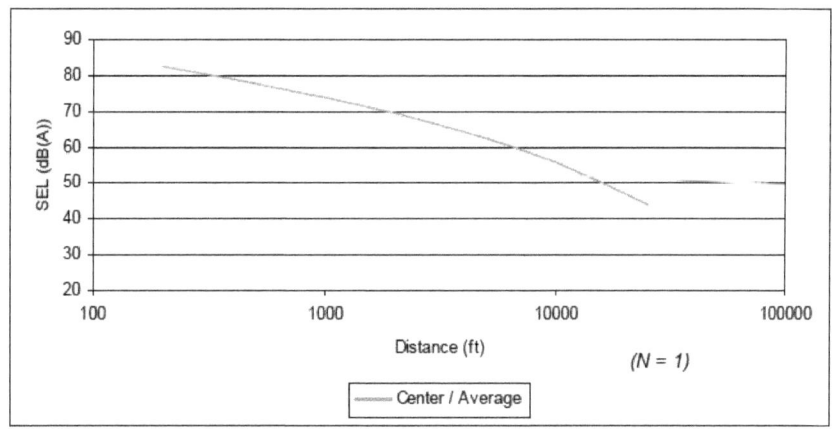

**Figure C-2. Reference L$_{AE}$-Versus-Distance Curves for INM, B206B
Corrected to 160 kts at 71.4 degrees F and 38.1 Percent RH**

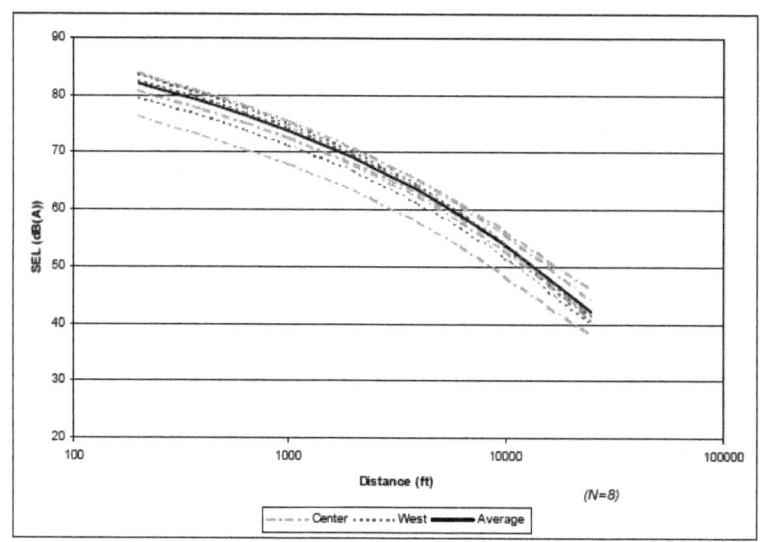

**Figure C-3. Reference L$_{AE}$-Versus-Distance Curves for INM, B206L
Corrected to 160 kts at 71.4 degrees F and 38.1 Percent RH**

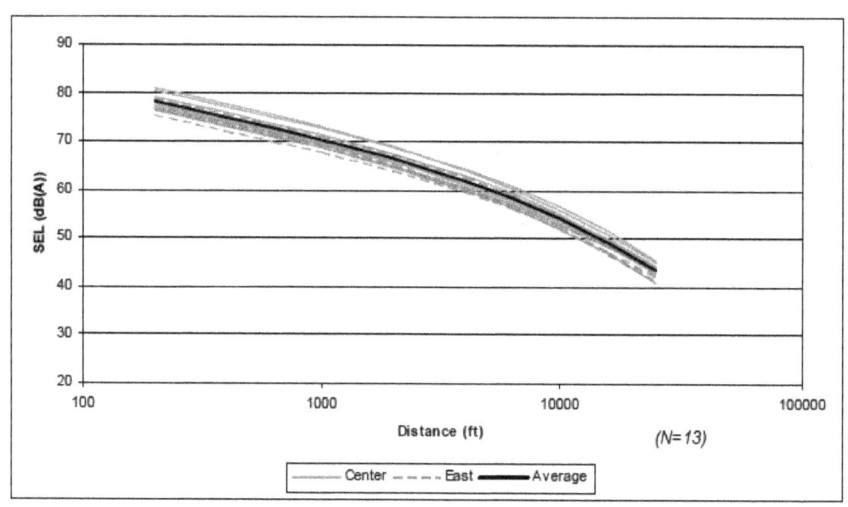

**Figure C-4. Reference L$_{AE}$-Versus-Distance Curves for INM, C207
Corrected to 160 kts at 71.4 degrees F and 38.1 Percent RH**

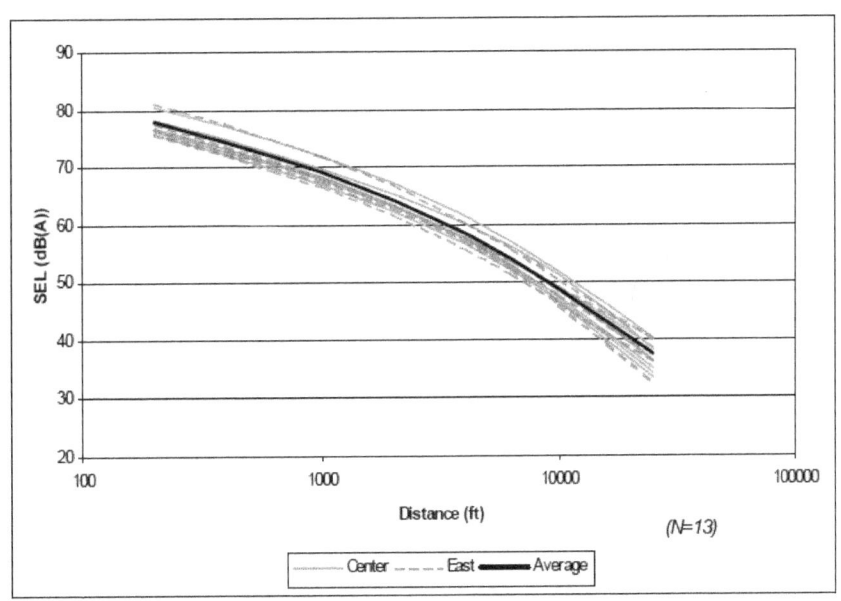

Figure C-5. Reference L$_{AE}$-Versus-Distance Curves for INM, DHC-6 Corrected to 160 kts at 71.4 degrees F and 38.1 Percent RH

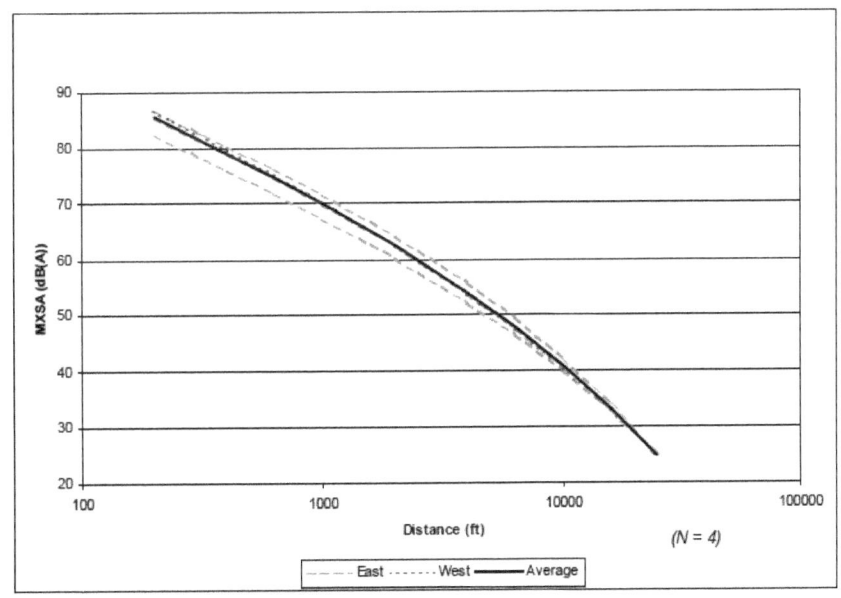

Figure C-6. Reference L$_{ASmx}$-Versus-Distance Curves for INM, AS350 Corrected to 71.4 degrees F and 38.1 Percent RH

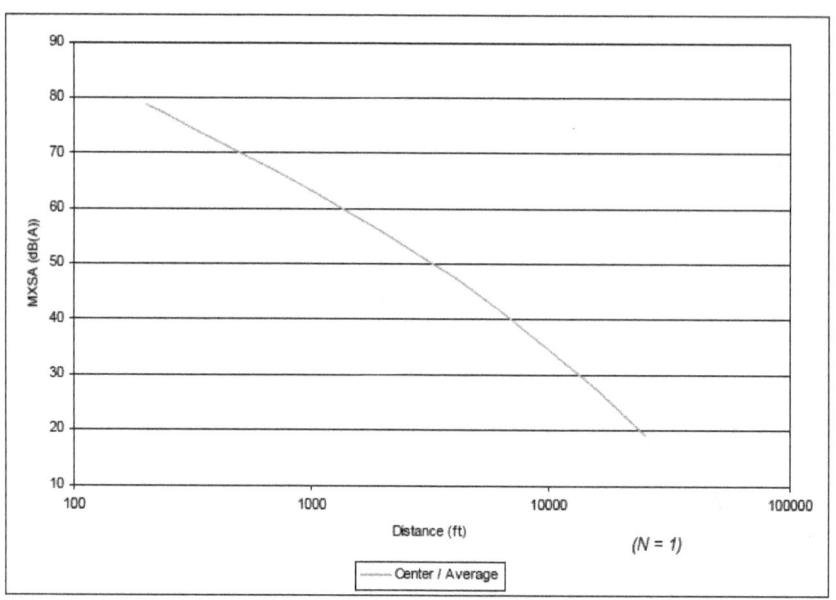

**Figure C-7. Reference L$_{ASmx}$-Versus-Distance Curves for INM, B206B
Corrected to 71.4 degrees F and 38.1 Percent RH**

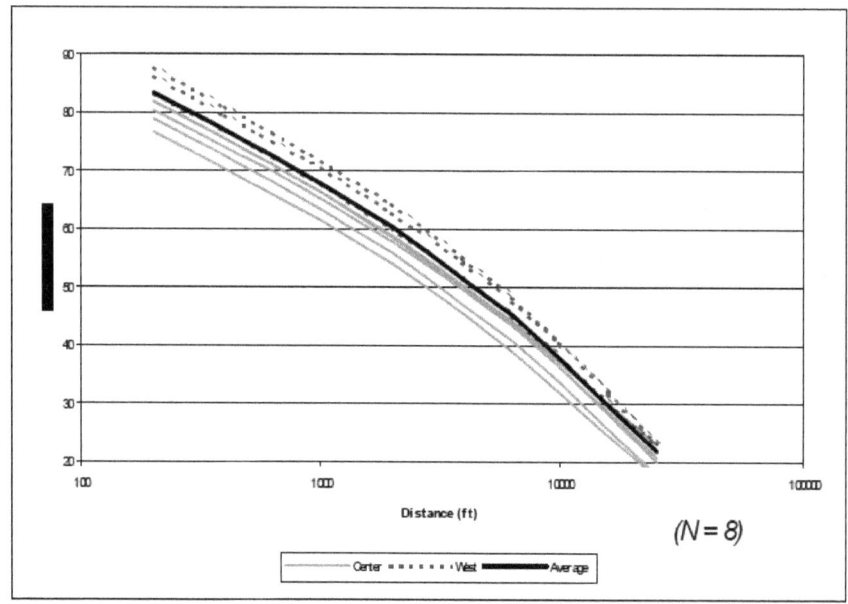

**Figure C-8. Reference L$_{ASmx}$-Versus-Distance Curves for INM, B206L
Corrected to 71.4 degrees F and 38.1 Percent RH**

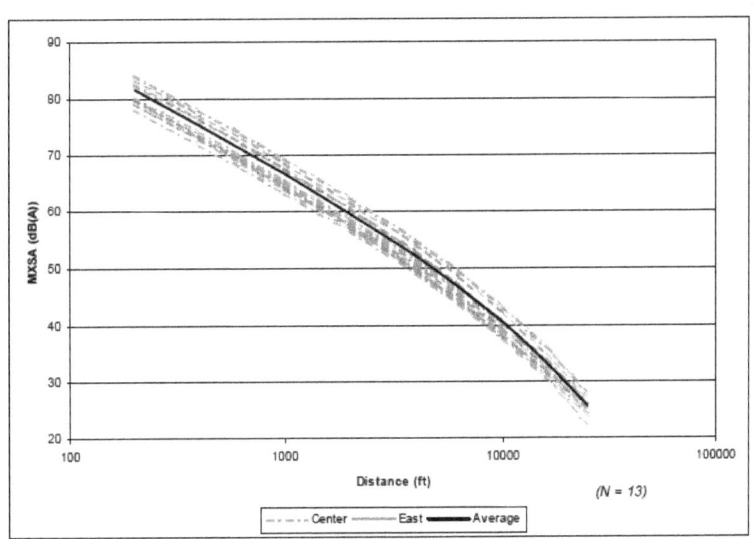

**Figure C-9. Reference L$_{ASmx}$-Versus-Distance Curves for INM, C207
Corrected to 71.4 degrees F and 38.1 Percent RH**

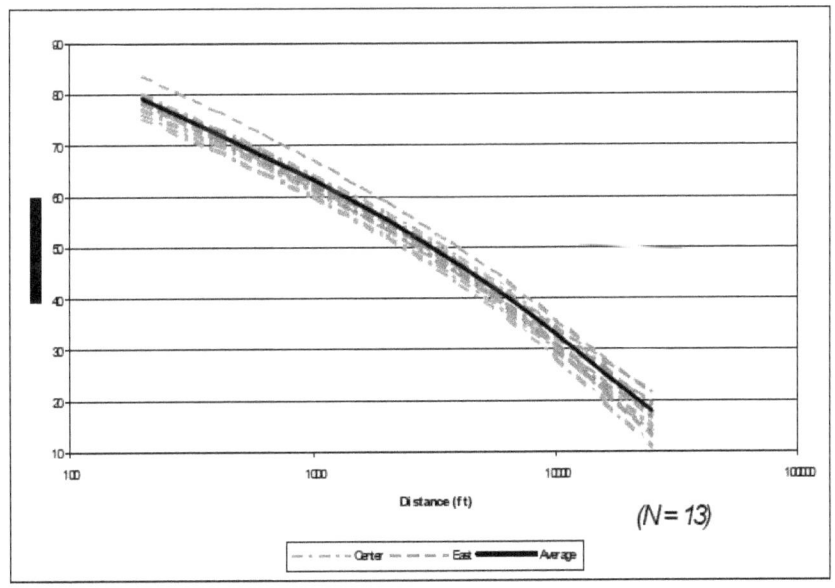

**Figure C-10. Reference L$_{ASmx}$-Versus-Distance Curves for INM, DHC-6
Corrected to 71.4 degrees F and 38.1 Percent RH**

Appendix D
NODSS Reference Spectral Data

This appendix presents the individual spectra for the 39 microphone events, along with the associated energy-averaged spectra. Figures D-1 through D-5 present these spectra for the AS350, B206B, B206L, C207 and DHC-6, respectively.

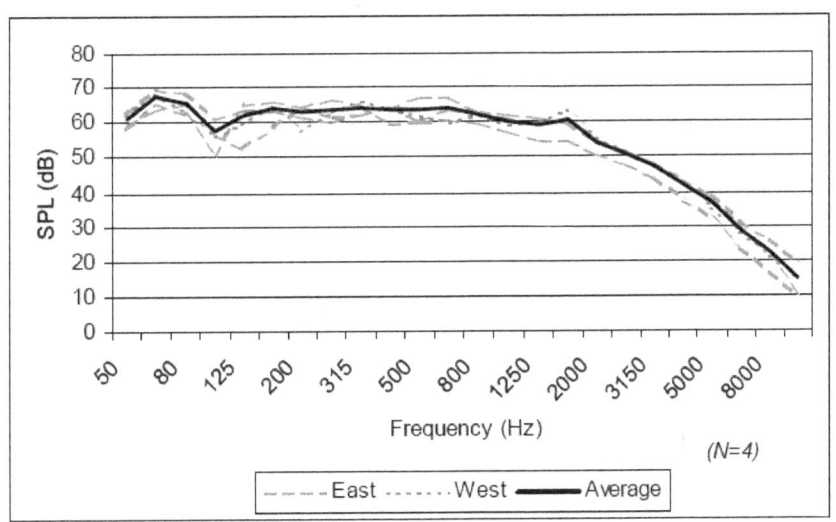

Figure D-1. Reference Spectra for NODSS, AS350
Corrected to 1000 ft at 71.4 degrees F and 38.1 Percent RH

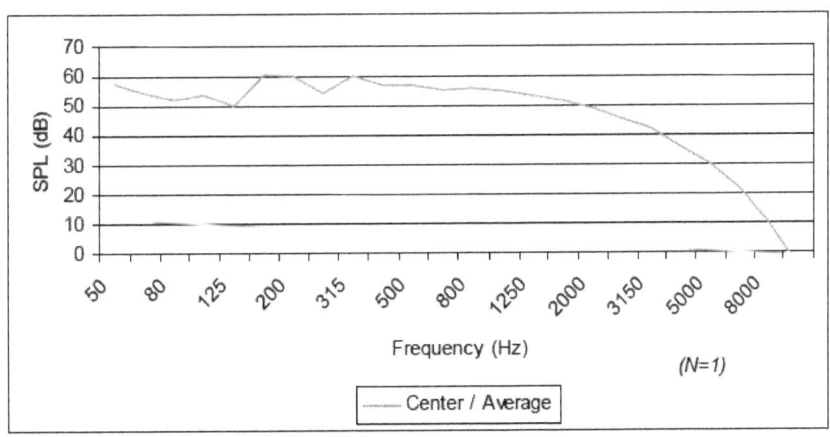

Figure D-2. Reference Spectra for NODSS, B206B
Corrected to 1000 ft at 71.4 degrees F and 38.1 Percent RH

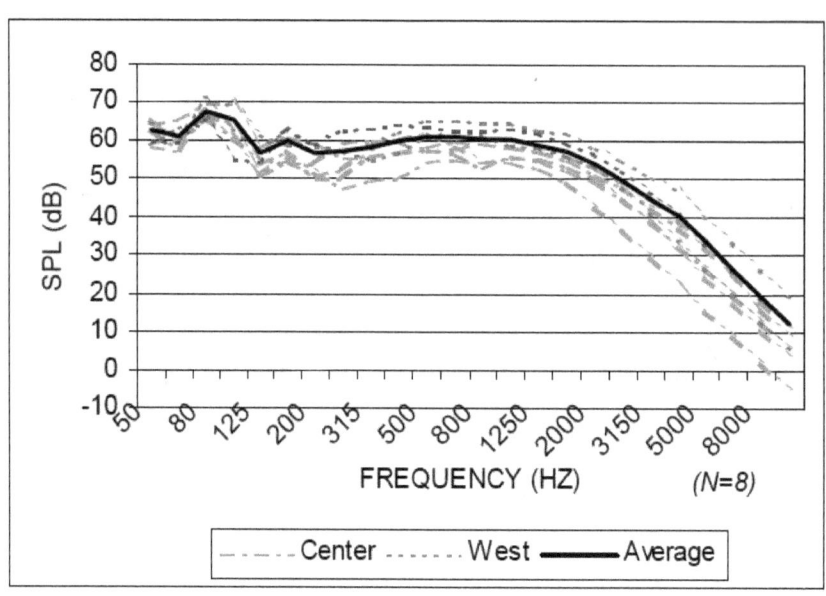

Figure D-3. Reference Spectra for NODSS, B206L
Corrected to 1000 ft at 71.4 degrees F and 38.1 Percent RH

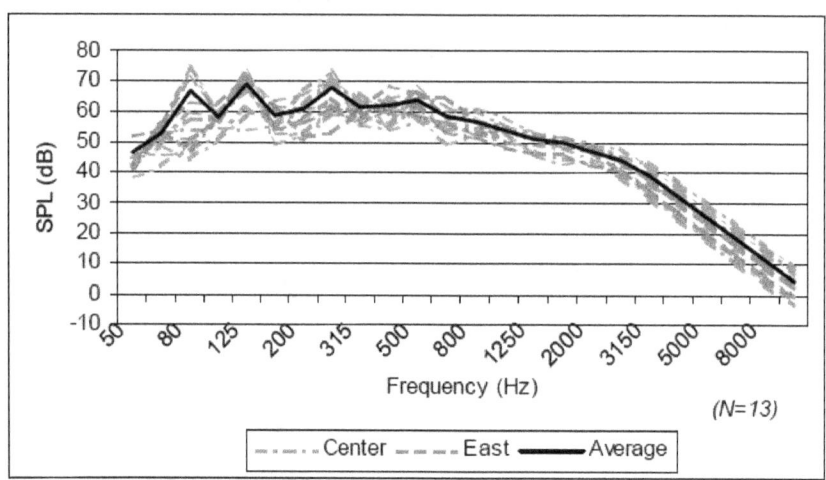

Figure D-4. Reference Spectra for NODSS, C207
Corrected to 1000 ft at 71.4 degrees F and 38.1 Percent RH

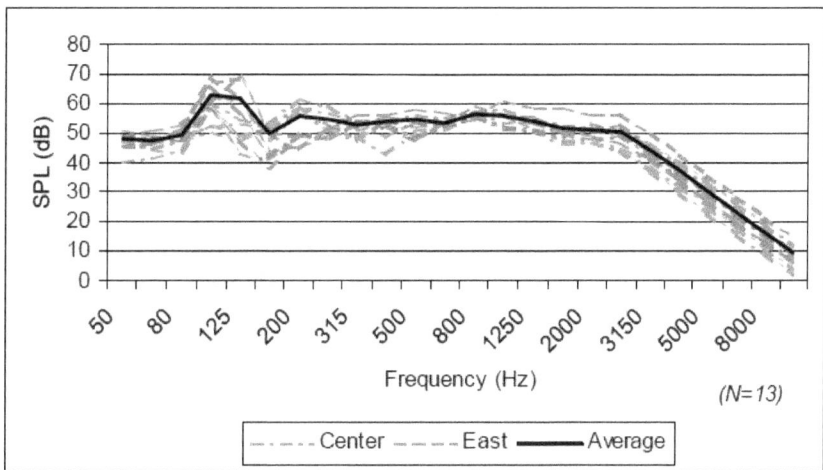

**Figure D-5. Reference Spectra for NODSS, DHC-6
Corrected to 1000 ft at 71.4 degrees F and 38.1 Percent RH**

www.ingramcontent.com/pod-product-compliance
Lightning Source LLC
Chambersburg PA
CBHW052019280526
45793CB00005B/1048